I0056842

Options Trading Strategies For Beginners

A Beginners Guide For Investing And Making Profits With Options, Swing And Day Trading

Byron McGrady

© **Copyright 2021 By Byron McGrady - All rights reserved.**

The content contained within this book may not be reproduced, duplicated or transmitted without direct written permission from the author or the publisher.

Under no circumstances will any blame or legal responsibility be held against the publisher, or author, for any damages, reparation, or monetary loss due to the information contained within this book. Either directly or indirectly.

Legal Notice:

This book is copyright protected. This book is only for personal use. You cannot amend, distribute, sell, use, quote or paraphrase any part, or the content within this book, without the consent of the author or publisher.

Disclaimer Notice:

Please note the information contained within this document is for educational and entertainment purposes only. All effort has been executed to present accurate, up to date, and reliable, complete information. No warranties of any kind are declared or implied. Readers acknowledge that the author is not engaging in the rendering of legal, financial, medical or professional advice. The content within this book has been derived from various sources. Please consult a licensed professional before attempting any techniques outlined in this book.

By reading this document, the reader agrees that under no circumstances is the author responsible for any losses, direct or indirect, which are incurred as a result of the use of information contained within this document, including, but not limited to, errors, omissions, or inaccuracies

Table of Contents

Introduction

You can make money out of trading options with anyone, whether you are a complete beginner or an experienced trader.

This is for those who are yet to find out about the market and are unsure how it all works. You will learn the market and how much profit can be made as a beginner.

The options market has been known for years and remains one of the most profitable and exciting investment opportunities available to us today. With technology constantly being developed, it's now easier than ever to trade options without worrying about complicated strategies or trading platforms.

Options are very different from stocks since they're designed as derivatives. That means that options are tied to an underlying asset (stock, index, or commodity) and are traded outside of their relationship with that asset. They're considered more speculative than conservative investments. Stocks were designed as equity investments, which means that they represent ownership in the firms that issue them. Even though you can't cash out your shares before they mature, they provide a reliable way to earn **passive income**.

This explains how, as an options trader, one can gain passive income. It is possible by using different strategies while trading options and also making profits through this. The strategies explained here are tested as profitable in the market, but one should apply common sense.

Options are a very popular and effective way to make money. However, options trading has become extremely complicated and complex over the years.

Investors use options to speculate whether they believe that a stock's price will go up over time. If the investor anticipates that stock to increase, they will buy an option to gain exposure to that increase. If they do not predict that the price will increase, they may sell their option.

If you're new to the world of options trading, there are a few things that you need to know before you begin trading. You have to learn the basics of options trading at the outset before moving on to a more detailed explanation of each option's characteristics.

You will learn what kind of option you should buy and how to trade it. This gives you an idea about how to trade options to manage your risk while making profits.

Remember this is not a complete guide on options trading. It is intended to give you a general idea of how options trading works. Before you begin trading options, it's important to know a little about what they are and how they work.

CHAPTER 1:

Fundamental Analysis

To make the best trades, you have to gather as much data as possible regardless of what market you are working in. There are two ways to get the most out of any of the data you gather, the first is via technical analysis, and the second is via fundamental analysis.

Fundamental analysis looks at specific factors based on the underlying asset for the market that you are working in.

Fundamental analysis is typically considered easier to master than concepts less expressly related to understanding market movement exclusively.

Fundamental Analysis Rules

The best time to use fundamental analysis is when you are looking to gain a broad idea of the state of the market as it stands and how that relates to the state of things shortly when it comes time to trading successfully.

Establish a Baseline

To begin analyzing the fundamentals, the first thing that you will need to do is to create a baseline regarding the company's overall performance.

To generate the most useful results possible, the first thing you will need to do is gather data both regarding the company in question and the related industry as a whole.

When gathering macro data, it is important to keep in mind that no market will operate in a vacuum, which means the reasons behind specific market movement can be much more far-reaching than they first appear. Fundamental analysis works because of the stock market's propensity for patterns. If you trace a specific market moved back to the source, you will have a better idea of what to keep an eye on in the future.

Furthermore, all industries go through several different phases where their penny stocks will be worth more or less overall based on general popularity. If the industry is producing many popular penny stocks, then overall volatility will be down while at the same time liquidity will be at an overall high.

Consider Worldwide Issues

Once you hold the current phase you are dealing with, the next thing you will want to consider is anything that is going on in the wider world that will after the type of businesses you tend to favor in your penny stocks. Not being prepared for major paradigm shifts, especially in penny stocks where new companies come and go so quickly, means that you can easily miss out on massive profits and should be avoided at all costs.

To ensure you are not blindsided by news you could have seen coming, it is important to look beyond the obvious issues that are consuming the 24-hour news cycle and dig deeper into the comings and goings of the nation's going to most directly affect your particular subsection of penny stocks.

One important worldwide phenomenon that you will want to pay specific attention to is anything in the realm of technology. Major paradigm shifts like the smartphone's adoption of electric cars' current move can create serious paradigm shifts.

Put It All Together

This is to compare what has been and what might to what the current state of the market is. Not only will this give you a realistic idea of what other investors are going to do if certain events occur the way they have in the past, but you will also be able to use these details to identify underlying assets that are currently on the cusp of generating the type of movement that you need if you want to utilize them via binary options trades.

The best time to get on board with a new underlying asset is when it is nearing the end of the post-bust period or the end of a post-boom period. Depending on if you are going to set a call or a put. You will have the greatest access to the freedom of the market, and thus, have access to the greatest overall allowable risk you will find in any market.

Remember, the amount of risk that you can successfully handle without an increase in the likelihood of failure will start decreasing as soon as the boom or bust phase begins in earnest, so it is important to get in as quickly as possible if you hope to maximize your profits truly.

Understand the Relative Strength of Any Given Trade

When an underlying asset is experiencing a boom phase, the strength of its related fundamentals will determine how other investors are going to act when it comes to binary options trading. Remember, when it comes to fundamental analysis, what an underlying asset looks like at the moment isn't nearly as important as what it is likely to look like in the future, and the best way to determine those details is by keeping an eye on the past.

Quantitative Fundamental Analysis

The sheer volume of data and a large number of varying numbers found in the average company's financial statements can easily be intimidating and bewildering for conscientious investors who are digging into them for the first time. You will quickly find that they are a goldmine of information when determining how likely a company is to continue producing reliable dividends in the future.

At their most basic, a company's financial statements disclose the information relating to its financial performance over a set period. Unlike qualitative concepts, financial statements provide cold, hard facts about a rarely open company for interpretation.

Important Statements

Balance Sheet

A balance sheet shows a detailed record of all of a company's equity, liabilities, and assets for a given period. A balance sheet shows a balance to a company's financial structure by dividing its equity by the combination of shareholders and liabilities to determine its current assets.

In this case, assets represent the resources that the company is actively in control of at a specific point in time. It can include things like buildings, machinery, inventory, cash, and more. It will also show the total value of any financing that has been used to generate those assets. Financing can come from either equity or liabilities. Liabilities include debt that must be paid back eventually, while equity, in this case, measures the total amount of money that its owners have put into the business. This can include profits from last years, which are known collectively as retained earnings.

Income Statement

It takes a closer look at the company's performance exclusively for a given timeframe. There is no boundary to the length of time an income statement considers, which means you could see them generated month to month or even day to day; however, the most common type used by public companies are either annual or quarterly. Income statements provide information on profit, expenses, and revenues that resulted from the business that took place over a specific period.

Cash Flow Statement

The cash flow statement frequently shows all of the cash outflow and inflow for the company over a given period. The cash flow statement often focuses on operating cash flow, which is the cash generated by day to day business operations. It will also include any cash that is available from investing, which is often used to invest in assets, along with any cash that might have been generated by long-term asset sales or the sale of a secondary business that the company previously owned. Cash due to financing is another name for money paid off or received based on issuing or borrowing funds.

The cash flow statements are quite important as it is often more difficult for businesses to manipulate them than many other financial documents. While accountants can manipulate earnings with ease, it is much more difficult to fake having access to cash in the bank where none exists. This is why many savvy investors consider the cash flow statement the most reliable way to measure a specific company's performance.

Finding the Details

While tracking down all the disparate financial statements on the company's you are considering purchasing stock in can be cumbersome, the Securities and Exchange Commission (SEC) requires all publicly traded companies to submit regular filings outlining all of their financial activities, including a variety of different financial statements. This also includes managerial discussions, reports from auditors, deep dives into the operations and prospects of upcoming years, and more.

These types of details can all be found in the 10-K filing that each company is required to file every year, along with the 10-Q filing that they must send out once per quarter. Both types of documents can be found online, both at the corporate website for the company and on the SEC website. As the version that hits the corporate site doesn't need to be complete, it is best to visit SEC.gov and get to know the Electronic Data Gathering, Analysis, and Retrieval (EDGAR) system automates the process of indexing, validating, collecting, forward, and accepting submissions. As this system was designed in the mid-90s, however, it is important to dedicate some time to learning the process as it is more cumbersome than 20 years of user interface advancements have to lead you to expect.

Qualitative Fundamental Analysis

Qualitative factors are generally less tangible and include name recognition, the patents it holds, and its board members' quality. Qualitative factors to consider include:

Business Model

The first thing that you will want to do when you catch wind of a company that might be worth following up on is to check out its business model, which is more or less a generalization of how it makes its money. You can typically find these sorts of details on the company website or in its 10-K filing.

Competitive Advantage

You have to consider the various competitive advantages that the company you have your eye on might have over its competition. Companies that will be successful in the long-term are always going to have an advantage over their competition in one of two ways. They can either have better operational effectiveness or improved strategic positioning. Operational effectiveness is the name given to doing the same things as the competition but more efficiently and effectively. Strategic positioning occurs when a company gains an edge by doing things that nobody else is doing.

Changes to the Company

To properly narrow down your search, you will typically find the most reliable results when it comes to companies that have recently seen major changes to their corporate structure as it is these types of changes that are likely to ultimately precede events that are more likely to see the company jump to the next level. The specifics of what happened in this instance are nearly as important as statistically speaking; 95% of companies that experience this type of growth started with a significant change to the status quo.

CHAPTER 2:

Before You Enter a Trade

You have to know a few things before you enter the market to understand how to filter out and consistently pick good trades.

Portfolio Balance

Before you do anything, you need to look at your portfolio balance first. When you're planning a new trade, it's always important to ask yourself why you need that trade and how it will affect your portfolio. Do you even really need it? For instance, if your portfolio already has plenty of bearish trades, it would generally be better for you to avoid adding more.

You need to reduce your risk in every situation, so the key here is to balance out your trades. That's how one develops a great portfolio, risk diversification. When you have many bearish trades in hand, look for bullish trades to offset the risk and vice versa. Once you internalize this, it becomes far easier to focus on your portfolio needs and filter out the rest from the first moment you start looking for a new trade.

Liquidity

Liquidity is straight-up one of the essential qualities of a good, tradable option. You don't want to remain with an illiquid option, no matter how lucrative it looks. Here's a simple rule to follow when looking for a new trade: for it to be a good trade, the underlying stock should be trading at least 100,000 shares daily. If the numbers are less than that, the trade isn't worth your time.

In a market as big and efficient as the one we have, the calculations only become more accurate over time. Similarly, when considering the underlying options, there should be a minimum of 1,000 open interest contracts for the strikes you are trading for it to be a good trade. It ensures quick entry into and exit from the market. Remember, liquidity is important.

Implied Volatility Percentile

When a trade satisfies the two criteria, it's time to move on to the next step—the IV percentile. You need to check how high or low the implied volatility of an option is, which is measured by using percentile scores. Let me explain with an example:

Say, if AAPL has IV of 35% but IV percentile of 70%, it means that while the current volatility is low, in the last year, it was higher than what it currently is (35%) for more than 70% of the time. So, the implied volatility for AAPL is relatively high, and you should be looking to employ premium-selling strategies.

Picking a Strategy

Picking a great strategy is as much a matter of eliminating as it is a matter of selecting, perhaps even more so. You can easily eliminate many strategies once you have a good idea of the IV and the IV percentile of the underlying stock and how it affects the options. For example, it's easy to eliminate strategies like debit spreads and long single options when you know the IV is high and the pricing rich. Then it's time to consider our risk tolerance and account size to pick the best strategy out of the ones left (iron condors, credit spreads, strangles, etc.).

Strikes and Month

Your trading style and goals also play a big part in how you decide to pick trades. Some people are more risk-averse than others, and that's okay. You should always select the right strategy based on the risk level you're comfortable with. If you're selling credit spreads, let's say, and you have the option to sell them at either a strike price that has a 90% chance of success of a strike price that has a 65% chance of success, you need to decide which option you want to go with based on the level of aggression you're comfortable with. It needs to fit your trading style and your goals.

You also need to do is give yourself sufficient time. This makes sure the trade can work out. This means that you should place low IV strategies at sixty–ninety days out and high IV strategies at thirty–sixty days out. You should read up on Theta value (one of the Greeks) and how it affects volatility.

Position Size

It is one of those areas where even some of the more experienced traders fail. You must understand this concept so you can make great trades often. Before placing a trade, you should always carefully assess your position size. As your trading position gets bigger, so does the risk, but this isn't linear, as many studies have shown. The risk increases exponentially, and one bad trade could easily lead to a blown account in this case. I strongly advise you to start with small positions as a beginner and continue to do so even when you're an intermediate. Your risk scale should be a sliding scale of 1–5% of your total balance on which all your trades need to be placed.

The cash or margin you use to cover a trade is what we call risk. For example, when selling a $1 wide credit put spread for 50 cents, you would need to cover it up with a $50 margin. You use this $50 margin to base your trade-off for each trade you make. If your account is worth $20,000 and you wish to allocate 3% of your account (it fits the 1–5% sliding scale criteria), you can take $600 of risk (3% of $20,000). You divide this by $50, and you get 12, which is the number of spreads you should sell at most. If this number is a fraction, always round down and never up.

Future Moves

You must've heard the popular saying that a chess grandmaster can foresee as many as 20 moves ahead. A good options trader also plans and foresees future moves. You're going to lose to the market more often than not if you're not thinking a few moves ahead. Always have another plan in case things go nasty and you need to shield yourself from losses.

And while shielding yourself from a losing trade is important, it's also important to plan how to turn a loss into a winning one.

Sometimes, you won't be able to make a winning trade. That's just how the market works; some trades go wrong no matter how well you plan. But you need to keep asking yourself important questions constantly. When you do this, your mind stays sharp and ready to jump into action to formulate a new plan or make an adjustment as and when the need arises.

CHAPTER 3:

Choosing a Broker

For selecting brokers, you have many options available. There are full-services, discounts, online, etc. Understanding the differences between them and selecting the ones best suited for your purposes is crucial if you wish to succeed. Another area that many beginners ignore and then receive a rude lesson in is the regulations surrounding options trading.

There aren't too many rules to comply with, but they have significant consequences for your capital and risk strategies.

Generally, there are two major varieties of brokers: discount and full-service. A lot of full-service brokers have discount arms these days so that you will see some overlap. Full-service refers to an organization where brokerage is just a part of a larger financial supermarket.

The broker might offer you other investment solutions, estate planning strategies, and so on. They'll also have an in-house research wing, which will send you reports to help you trade better. Besides this, they'll also have phone support if you have questions or wish to place an order.

Make a good relationship with them, a full-service broker will become a good organization to network. Every broker loves a profitable customer since it helps with marketing. A full-service broker will have good relationships in the industry, and if you have specific needs, they can help you with the right people.

The price of all this service is you paying higher commissions than average. It is up to you to see whether this is a good price for you to pay. You need not sign up with a full-service broker to trade successfully. Order matching is done electronically, so it's not as if a person on the floor can get you a better price these days. Therefore, a full-service house will not give you better execution.

Discount brokers, on the other hand, are all about focus. They help you trade, and that is it. At least not intentionally, they will not advise from a business perspective, and phone ordering is nonexistent. That doesn't mean they reduce customer service.

Margin

Margin refers to the number of assets you currently hold in your account. Your assets are cash and positions. As the market value of your positions fluctuates, so does the amount of margin you have. Margin is an important concept to grasp since it is at the core of your risk management discipline.

You must make a choice when you open an account with your broker.

You can open either a cash or margin account. To trade options, open a margin account. Briefly, a cash account does not include leverage within it, so all you can trade are stocks. There are no account minimums for a cash account, and even if they are, they're minuscule.

A margin account is subject to weird rules. First, the minimum balances for a margin account are higher. Most brokers will impose a $10,000 minimum, and some will even increase this amount based on your trading style. The account minimum achieves nothing by itself, but it acts as a broker's commission.

The thinking is that with this much money on the line, the person trading will be more serious about it and won't blow it away. If only it worked like that. Anyway, the minimum balance is a hard and fast rule. Another rule you should know is the Pattern Day Trader (PDT) designation.

PDT is a rule that comes directly from the SEC. We classify anyone who executes four or more orders within five days as a PDT ("Pattern Day Trader," 2019). Once this tag is slapped onto you, your broker will ask you to post at least $25,000 in the margin as a minimum balance. Again, this minimum balance does nothing, but the SEC figures that if you screw up, this gives you enough of a buffer.

Margin Call

One other aspect of margin you must understand is the margin call. This is a dreaded message for most traders, including institutional ones.

The purpose of all risk management is to keep you as far away as possible from this ever happening to you. A margin call is issued when you have inadequate funds in your account to cover its requirements.

Remember that your margin is the combination of the cash you hold plus the value of your positions.

If you have $1,000 in cash, but your position is currently in a loss of -$900, you'll receive a margin call to post more cash to cover the potential loss you're headed for. You'll receive it well in advance. If you don't post more margins, your broker has the right to close out your positions and recover whatever cash they can to stop their risk limits from being triggered.

The threshold beyond which your broker will issue a margin call is called the maintenance margin. Usually, you need to maintain 25% of your initial position value (that is: when you enter a position) as cash in your account. Most brokers have a handy indicator that tells you how close you are to the limit.

The leading cause of margin calls is leverage. You can borrow money with a margin account and use that to boost your returns. Let's look at an example: If you trade with $10,000 of your own money and borrow $20,000 from your broker to enter a position, you control $30,000 worth of the position. Let's say this position makes a gain of $10,000 to bring its total value to $40,000.

You've just made a 100% return on this investment (since you invested only $10,000), although the total return on the position is 33% (10,000/30,000). What happens if you lose $10,000 on the position, though? Well, you just lost 100% despite the position losing only 33%. Leverage is a double-edged sword.

It is far too simplistic to call leverage bad or good. It is what it is. If you're a beginner, you should not be borrowing money to trade under any circumstances. When you're experienced, you can do so as much as you want. Please note the difference between the leverage where you borrow money and the leverage options provide.

A single contract gives you control over a larger pie of stock with options, but the option premium still needs to be paid. It is, therefore, cheaper to trade options than the common stock. If you were to borrow money to pay for the option premium, then you're indulging in foolish behavior, and you need to step away.

There's a difference between leverage being inherent within the instrument's structure and using leverage to increase the amount of something you can buy—the latter when you're a beginner.

Execution

A favorite pastime of unsuccessful traders is to complain about execution. Their losses are always the broker's fault, and if it weren't for the greedy brokers, they'd be rolling in the dough, diving in and out of it like Scrooge McDuck. Complaining about your execution will get you nothing.

A big reason for these complaints is that most beginner traders don't realize that the price they see on the screen is not the same as what is being traded on the exchange.

We live in an era of high-frequency trading, and the markets' smallest measurement of time has gone from second to microseconds. Trades are constantly pouring in, and the matching engine is always finding suitable sellers for buyers. Given the pace of the market, it is important to understand that it is impossible to figure out an instrument's exact price.

Therefore, within your risk management plan, you must make allowance for high volatility times when the fluctuations will be bigger. For now, I want you to understand that just because the price you received differed from what was on screen doesn't mean the broker is incompetent.

Price Quotes

Many traders are stumped when they first look at their trading screens and see that there are two prices for everything. After all, every financial channel always displays one price for security, but you'll be quoted two different prices within the price box when trading. This is a small but crucial detail for you to understand.

The lower price you receive is called the bid, and this is the price you will pay if you sell the instrument. The higher price is asked, and this is what you will pay to buy the instrument.

The single price you see on your TV screen is the "Last Traded Price" or LTP. Don't think the LTP is the actual price since the market moves constantly.

Even the spread (the difference between ask and the bid) doesn't accurately reflect the genuine state of things thanks to constant movement. Just remember to look at the spread to understand what you'll be paying. The spread increases and contracts constantly, but if you see that it is getting too big, this is a sign that too much volatility exists, and you're better off staying out.

CHAPTER 4:

Options Trading Platforms

A trading platform is the most important feature of a broker, which you will use to trade.

Many of us do not usually take this issue into account, and we only look at commissions. Still, as necessary as the broker service itself is the trading platform it offers us.

Why? Because the failure or success of our investment depends mainly on the power and reliability of the tool.

A trading platform and broker are not the same.

The broker is the midway that acts directly between us and the stock market. On the other hand, the trading platform is the work tool (software) through which we will operate and launch orders.

Thus, the broker will offer us a service while the platform will allow us to execute our strategy. Therefore, if the investment platform is not right, we can have serious problems when trading.

When hiring an online broker, we are going to come across two possibilities:

- Brokers who have developed their trading platform.

- Brokers using a multi-broker platform (also available to other providers).

Although there are powerful tools developed in-house by some brokers, keep in mind that a multi-broker platform can open many doors for you when it comes to trading and trading with other brokers.

- **Find the best trading platform:** There are some criteria you must take into account to choose a trading software:

- **Offer the instruments with which you want to invest:** Not all systems offer trading with any instrument.

- **The platform should be friendly and easy to use:** The best platform suggests the most comfortable and most intuitive usability for the user. With possibilities on the market, it makes no sense to continue using a complicated idea that is comprehensive.

- **Access to the tool code:** Some platforms such as MetaTrader 4 allow you to modify the programming code to create your indicators or scripts, among others.

Different Platforms

These are some of the top options trading platforms in the market today.

Firstrade

It is an online investment company that offers one of the best options trading platforms on the market. It became one of the first companies to launch into online trading when it launched in 1997 under First Flushing Securities.

The company changed its name to Firstrade a year later and has since been a pillar of online investing.

Competitive costs per order: Firstrade does not have the lowest fixed cost per order of the best options brokers on our list, but at a base rate of $6.95 and $0.75 per contract, it remains competitive.

Extended opening hours: One advantage of trading options with Firstrade is its ability to trade extended hours. This feature allows you to jump into exchanges likely to be affected by recent developments in the hours before and after exchanges on the standard market.

If you read something in the morning news that made you want to place a pre-market operation, you can do it between 8:05 and 9:25 a.m. with Firstrade.

Are you interested in participating in the aftermarket? You can do this too with Firstrade. It will allow you to place orders from 4:05 p.m. to 5:25 p.m.

TradeKing

It is an online broker found in 2005 and part of the TradeKing Group, Inc. It is merged with its sister company Zecco Trading.

Notable features of TradeKing: In recognition of excellence and excellence in customer service, TradeKing has received numerous awards over the years. Some of them include:

- Ranked 2019 Best in Class for Commissions and Fees by Stockbrokers.com

- Rated four stars by Barron Online corridor survey between 2006–2016

- Stockbrokers.com 2019 #1 innovation broker for its TradeKing Live platform

- Ranked # 1 in the merchant community for 2013–2014 according to the survey conducted by StockBrokers.com

Main base rates and competitive commissions: The base rate for TradeKing is $4.95. It only competes with OptionsHouse by offering the lowest base rate for the cost-conscious options trader.

And while TradeKing's $0.65 contract fees are not the lowest in the industry, they remain incredibly competitive with lesser-known companies.

However, compared to large companies, TradeKing rates offer a distinct advantage. These general cost-saving advantages make TradeKing the solution of choice for the best options broker.

All-in-one options trading platform: TradeKing software gives you everything you need on a fully functional trading platform. It hosts a page in its education center that specializes in options trading. This page presents options trading tools, option strategies, and on-demand videos to deepen your knowledge of options. Bank and make the most of TradeKing technology.

TradeStation

TradeStation is an online options trading platform offered by TradeStation Group, Inc. and TradeStation Securities, Inc.

The TradeStation group is located in Plantation, Florida. It is a subsidiary of Monex Group, Inc., located in Japan. It is considered the best broker because of its flexibility.

It has been known across as one of the best buy and sell options. Some of the awards and distinctions that the software has received include:

- Highest rating by Barron in the category Best for large merchants 2016

- Stockbrokers.com rewarded for the best platform technology 2012–2016

- Best in class from Stockbrokers.com for Mobile Trading 2016

- The top five online brokers in Business Daily 2016

Flexible and staggered price structure: You may think that option trading platforms of the type offered by TradeStation are reserved for high volume professional traders. While professional operators can use the TradeStation platform, TradeStation has enabled its software to benefit even those who do not trade as often.

You can do this thanks to its tiered price structure. Depending on your operations' frequency and volume, you can take advantage of a contract or a business plan.

By contract, it is better for rare merchants or those who do not work with large volumes. You pay a lump sum of $1.00 per contract with no base rate applicable. However, a minimum of a contract is required.

Those of you who can trade as "whales" are bets. They save money with the operating price plan.

Under this plan, you pay underlying fees for each transaction, as well as contract fees. These rates vary in volume. The higher the amount, the lower the rate.

For example, if you execute more than 200 transactions per month, your base is $4.99 plus $0.20 per contract. Fewer operations result in higher costs. The following key details the full price structure of TradeStation:

- Base of $4.99 plus $0.20/contract for 200 transactions/month.

- Base of $5.99 plus $0.30/contract for 100–199 transactions/month.

- Base of $6.99 plus $0.40/contract for 30–99 operations/month.

- Base of $7.99 plus $0.50/contract for 10–29 operations/month.

- Base of $9.99 plus $0.70/contract for 1–9 operations/month.

Trading at the base rate of $9.99 ($10.69 total) with TradeStation is not as profitable as some of its competitors, as shown in the table above. Even in this case, the price of TradeStation remains very competitive.

However, when you exceed this base rate, the comparison table clearly shows that TradeStation is the most profitable option than the most critical company names. This is true regardless of the volume.

OptionStation Pro

TradeStation set out to create the best platform for trading options, and there is no doubt that it has become one of the leaders in the online options trading industry. It is a powerful and feature-rich platform that allows you to take control of your options trading. Some of the benefits you get with OptionStation Pro include:

- Ability to quickly discover and classify potential business opportunities.

- Use a pre-established strategy to reduce the time between the discovery and execution of the transaction.

- Create, analyze, and track almost all option positions.

- Place one-click orders directly from an options chain.

- Fully customizable interface, which includes position management, dispersion types, graphic screens, etc.

TradeStation Mobile

It has been ranked among the best options brokers by the variety of access points offered to its customers.

You can still view appointments, view charts and tables, view data continuously in real-time, and execute operations. Not only that, but you can easily track locations and closely monitor your watch lists, among other features.

Other Notable Platforms

- Plus500

- eToro

- Capital.com

- IG

- XTB

- OANDA

- OptionsHouse

CHAPTER 5:

Passive Income

Making passive nature of income by using options trading might sound like a real dream. But, can it be turned into reality? To answer this very question, we first need to learn about the various aspects of active income and passive income to understand the major differences between the two. Right after that, we will be exploring some ways in which passive income can be generated by using various techniques of trading.

Passive money is the money generated regularly, which requires very little effort right on the recipient's side to maintain the same. Gains on interests, stocks, lottery winnings, commodities, and capital are often the earning types in mind. But this fits the most popular definition of passive income; there are still some countries that impose a definition of technical nature for passive income for the very purpose of taxation.

Active Trading vs. Passive Trading

Various people often ask about stock trading as being a source of passive income or not. The active nature of traders will be investing a great amount of effort and time in turning a profit. Well, their activity of the trade will be taken as the primary form of focus.

In the case of passive income, the earnings are derived from a limited partnership, rental property, or by using other enterprises, in short, anything in which any individual is not involved actively. Passive income is generally taxable. So, suppose you are looking out for generating passive income by using options. In that case, you must hand over the capital to a broker whom you trust, any automated system, or by investing your capital through copy trading.

Passive Income Pros and Cons

Right before we start with the various techniques of earning passive income by using options, it is very important to first learn about the benefits of passive income and its drawbacks. An obvious benefit related to passive income is the limited amount of time you will have to commit. But this also indicates the extreme pressure on the decisions of investments that you are going to make. Passive trading might sometimes end up in a very slow profit stream when you compare it with active trading. There are also certain dangers that you are most likely to oversee while monitoring your income. Ultimately, this might result in losing a great amount of potential profit.

Techniques for Generating Passive Income

There are some ways in which passive income can be made:

Automation

To make the whole game of passive income a lot easier, some people often opt for automation. When used properly, the automated systems can make you capable of generating substantial nature of profits. This is because there is only a specific trade number that one can make in a day. A unique algorithm can easily enter and exit the positions as soon as the pre-determined criteria have been met.

They will also permit you to trade in several markets at one time. Right after you have successfully programmed your criteria, passive income can also be generated while sleeping. Some of you might doubt the capabilities and efficiency of this system. But, around 75% of the trades made on New York and NASDAQ's stock exchange originate from all these algorithms and define their efficacies.

Software

Right before you start having passive income by using automated trading, you must lookout for the perfect software. Try doing your research, and never forget to check the assessments first before you start investing. Once done with your research, and you have chosen your software, you must develop a great strategy. You can start by creating a small checklist for your parameters of trading.

You can easily consider these:

- When to enter positions and when to exit them.

- Size of the position.

- Trading timeframe.

- Stop losses and targets.

Backtesting

Before starting any automated system for generating passive income from options, you will need to backtest the strategy first. This will permit you to test the entire system right before you risk in your capital. You need to run the software you chose right against any historical price data to gauge how efficiently it performs. You can easily identify the issues, if there are any, and fix them before investing.

Copy Trading

Another great way of developing passive income is by the method of copy trading. In place of giving in all your energy and time for developing the strategy and monitoring all the tasks, you can easily benefit by following the experienced traders' success. You need to select a trader, and a program will then be mimicking the trader's buying and selling by using your capital. But it might happen that the traders will take a minimal percentage of the profit that you make.

But it also comes along with certain drawbacks:

- Risking your capital: You need to be always prepared because of the market volatility. You might also lose the entire capital you have invested in. If you are risk-averse and if you cannot see yourself with huge losses, it is better not to opt for this option.

- Choosing a trader: Picking a trader might turn out to be a challenge. Any aggressive nature of options trader can clear you out within several days. Always consider the instrument of approach and choice that they use. You are also required to check the updated history of the trade of the trader. All you are looking out for is a consistent and steady form of results.

- Not keeping up with the trades proportionally: Certain sites might not permit you to trade proportionally. But, for good, the traders, most of the time, invest only in particular quantities. So, you need to ensure that you only focus on copying the trader.

Using Put-Selling Strategy

It is often regarded as the most efficient way of developing passive income. The best strategy that can be used is by buying stocks when they are overvalued instead of being undervalued. As you sell puts that are overvalued, you can rake in huge premiums from the buyers. You can also determine the option value based on the implied volatility of the same. Implied volatility can help in measuring the amount of greed and fear that is priced into any option.

When the implied volatility is considerably high, the prices of the options will tend to be overvalued. This can easily attract many investors.

The stocks that are your own will be trading much above the strike price for the duration of the option's lifespan. This indicates that you will be collecting the option's premium, and you are not required to purchase any of the underlying stocks. While this is taken as an ideal scenario, there are other scenarios for you to understand.

When the underlying stocks fall under the right level in the middle of the strike price and strike price that is less than the option's premium is the second scenario. The investor will be winning as the adjusted cost basis is better than the one currently present in the market, right after considering the received premium of the option.

The third scenario is when the stock price goes below a point below the strike price, subtracting the option's premium. This is often taken as the worst-case scenario for any trader of cash-secured put.

How You Can Make Money by Selling Puts?

Selling puts will be allowing you to set the stock strike price according to you at which you want to buy it. Selling puts is much more attractive than selling covered calls as you are not required to post your capital, which is beneficial for purchasing the shares. You need to follow certain steps right before selling the puts:

- Finding out a stock that you would like to buy.

- Deciding the entry price that you want to buy the shares.

- Evaluating the implied volatility.

- Setting the risk parameters.

CHAPTER 6:

Technical Indicators

What are technical indicators? These are useful indicators that provide information about trends and even possible turning points in stocks and securities prices. Technical indicators are among the tools used by traders and even analysts to predict the best times to purchase or sell stocks and options. The technical indicators also indicate the cycles.

A technical analyst will calculate the essential particulars of a stock. Many of the technical indicators are calculated using data such as:

- Closing price.

- Highs.

- Lows.

- Trading volumes.

- Opening prices.

- Among others.

Stock prices from the past couple of trades provide most of the raw data required to work out technical indicators. Data mostly used is often from the last thirty days.

The data is then utilized to develop a chart or trend that indicates what has been happening and what will happen to a particular stock. This is because past performance is a great indicator of future trends.

Options traders widely use technical indicators to predict the future movement of the price movement of stocks. They also indicate trends within the market. When it comes to technical indicators, there are two main types. These are:

1. Lagging Indicators

Lagging indicators are indicators that closely monitor and follow a stock's price pattern. This is why they are called lagging. These indicators are solely based on the last data. They are hence excellent at indicating any trend developing in the market or if a stock has entered a trading range. Lagging indicators can, for instance, point to a stock with a major downward trend and will most probably continue falling.

Future Trends and Pullbacks

Keep in mind that lagging indicators are not recommended when it comes to predicting future pullbacks or rallies. These indicators can indicate the trends that have developed until the latest point. However, they cannot point to future trends or events, even just for the following couple of days. Some common lagging indicators popularly used by options traders include ADX indicators, the Moving Average, and the MACD.

Therefore, lagging indicators are excellent at pointing at the developing trends but are poor at predicting or forecasting future stock price movement.

2. Leading Indicators

The other very useful technical indicators are the leading indicators. These technical indicators are beneficial at predicting future events. They often provide relevant information regarding possible crashes and future price gains. Some of the leading indicators include momentum indicators. These are capable of predicting or gauging the momentum of the price movements of a stock.

Momentum indicators are more like tossing a football in the air. No matter how high the ball rises, we know that it will eventually fall back to the ground. We may not know when it will stop going up, but we are sure that it will do so at one point. This is the genesis of momentum indicators.

Leading indicators such as the momentum indicators are excellent at revealing if a stock price has gone too far down or too high up. They also let us know whether there is a reduction in the momentum of the price movement. When the price moves too high, it simply means there has been an over-purchase of the stock. In such cases, then, the stock has been overbought.

Should the price move too low, then this says an oversupply of the stock, and buyers are possibly dropping it. If the stock has been overbought or oversold, it will not remain in this state for long. We can, therefore, make a deduction that a pullback is likely to happen. Most momentum indicators and the RSI are good examples of leading indicators.

Lagging and Leading Indicators

Most traders appreciate both lagging and leading indicators because they are both invaluable. You are informed of any possible price pullbacks and slowdowns as a trader. Ideally, you should never rely on just one of these indicators but both. This way, your predictions, and trades will always be accurate and reliable.

Most indicators sometimes produce false signals occasionally. Since this is a risk that you want to avoid, we recommend using at least two or three different indicators. Identify 3 specific indicators that you like, and if they all give you positive information about a stock, you can feel confident enough to invest in it. There are essentially hundreds of different indicators in use across the world. Most seasoned traders will have developed their technical indicators to predict the markets accurately. You should learn how to use about 5 different technical indicators. This way, you will have a wide variety of options to choose from.

Top Technical Indicators

We have noted above that there are hundreds of different technical indicators currently in use. However, some are absolutely crucial for options traders. If you can learn how to use about 5 of them, you will have a strong foundation for your technical analysis. Here is a look at some of the more important ones:

Average Directional Index Indicator, ADX

The ADX or average directional index is a popular indicator that is mostly used for confirmation purposes.

It essentially works to confirm the information or signals that are produced by other indicators. This technical indicator works by measuring the strength of any given trend. For example, you can use the ADX to measure if an upward trend or maybe even a downward trend is slowing down or gaining momentum.

This average directional index, ADX, combines the positive directional indicator, +DI, and the negative directional indicator, -DI. The -DI or negative directional indicator tracks the downward trend, while the +DI or positive directional tracks the upward trend in the stock market. When these two indicators are combined together, we get the Average Directional Index.

This combination of two strong indicators produces one powerful and unified trend strength indicator.

The +DI is showcased as a green line in the chart above, while the –DI is shown as a red line. The ADX indicator itself is shown as a fat black line. We note that there was a strong stock trend from late February until mid-April, as indicated by the ADX. The stock was trending upwards.

It is possible to notice that the ADX indicator never went below the 20 marks. This is a clear indicator of when the stock ever traded flat. An accurate assessment is mostly visible from the stock price. In general, we notice that this is an accurate assessment as it is visible from the strike price. There was a remarkable uptrend for the first three months and the last three months indicate a downward trend.

Oscillating Indicator

The ADX technical indicator also happens to be oscillating. Its oscillations range from zero to a hundred, with zero representing flat trades while a hundred represents a plunging or rising stock. Please note that the ADX indicator showcases the strength of a trend only without pointing its direction.

Also, the ADX values often range between 20 and 40. Rarely will you see ADX values above 60. The reason is that high values above 60 point to a trend that usually appears when there is a long recession or a long bull run. Any values that are below 20 often point to a stock entering the trading range.

According to our chart above, we notice that signals produced by the Average Directional Index, or ADX, indicator, any move that is way below 40 points and above will indicate the trend's slowdown. The options strategies always rely on large volumes of shares, so a trend that is slowing down is undesirable. Therefore, as a trader, if you notice any ADX indicator is a simple pointer, the trend is slowing down, and that now would be the best time to buy out.

Similarly, any index indicator that moves above 20 indicates that the sideways trading strategies are over because a new trend is currently developing. It is an indication that the current upward trend is almost drawing to an end. As such, it is time to make a positive movement that can be either bullish or bearish. Also, sometimes the ADX indicator can move way above 20. This is always a clear indication that the current upward trend has started to fade.

Again, in our chart above, the ADX technical indicator produced a signal right in the middle of April. You should learn how to look for stuff and be observant. Signals on this example can be obtained by observing and noting where there is. When the +DI, green, and wring signal process above +61422 –5840364. When the two indicators, the +DI, and the –DI cross paths with each other, we will identify our signal here. When they meet together, they should form a bullish signal. You should, therefore, always base your investment opportunity on recommendations from the map. Experts advise that you make use of only one or additionally two types of indicators. This way, you will be sure of what to do and when to do it.

Bollinger Band Strategies

Another technical strategy that is commonly used to showcase the voracity of stocks is the Bollinger strategy. There will always be an opportunity to learn from the boss. A Bollinger Band strategy or theory is mostly meant to showcase how volatile the stocks are.

This is a simple technical indicator as it is composed of a simple moving average and both its upper and lower bands. These upper and lower bands are only about 2 standard deviations away.

We can confidently say that standard deviation is more like statistical tools. This is because the majority of movement occurs around these positions. When you use the Bollinger Band theory, you will discover that it only works as a guide or gauge and should, therefore, be used in conjunction with other indicators. If you learn how to apply these indicators, then you stand a great chance for success.

The Bollinger Band theory operates optimally in conjunction with the twenty-day SMA or simple moving averages. We also need the standard deviations of the twenty-day SMA to create the Bollinger Bands. Some of the strategies that emanate from this indicator include long-term and short-term Bollinger Bands. The shorter-term bands which are less than twenty days are highly sensitive to price movement while the longer-term bands that exceed twenty days are less sensitive and more conservative.

CHAPTER 7:

Daily Routine for a Trader

Missteps occur in options trading. They regularly happen because an excessive amount of data is coming in without a moment's delay. You feel over-burden, froze, and forceful, or they frequently happen during calm/bring times when your watchman is down. Furthermore, there are constantly irregular mix-ups, for example, hitting an inappropriate catch—purchase rather than sell—or putting out an inappropriate position size. Such blunders can even occur with robotized methodologies.

Before each trading day, take a couple of minutes to experience a multi-day trading routine to help limit mistakes for the day. Here are the means to experience. Contingent upon the market you exchange, you may wish to include a couple of extra advances. This entire procedure takes a few minutes, however, spares you a great deal of dissatisfaction and cash.

Conditions in the Market

Make a brisk appraisal of trading conditions up until now. Is the pre-advertise demonstrating a great deal of instability, or is it steady? Is there a pattern or explicit propensities you take note of?

Such an evaluation tells you how to continue and whether you ought to exchange your framework by any stretch of the imagination. This is particularly significant if utilizing an emotional framework—a framework that fluctuates marginally dependent on economic situations. For instance, in unpredictable conditions, you may have a bigger expected benefit focus than on a multi-day when there is no unpredictability.

Keep Notes

On your graph, put content notes expressing when high effect news discharges are. Whenever fascinated in exchange, you may disregard one of these occasions, which could cost you beyond all doubt. Record it on your diagram. If the occasion happens later in the day, look over and put the content note close to the declaration's estimated time. That way, you will see it when the opportunity arrives.

Launch Platform Is Vital

Dispatch your stage. Ensure statements are gushing (not slacking or sporadic), and the program is running easily. Most intermediaries give dependable information encourages, yet issues can emerge. If the information feed is irregular or appears to be erroneous, don't exchange until the issue is fixed. On the off chance that it looks right, continue.

Automated Strategies Should Be Confirmed

Regardless of whether your day exchange physically, you may have some robotized orders. For instance, in Ninja Trader and Meta Trader, you can convey stop misfortune requests and focuses on the minute you enter a position.

Ensure these stop misfortune requests and targets are set properly. If trading with a "robot," ensure all settings are exact before beginning it.

Have an End Time

If you see a time you pattern to give back benefits all the time, compose a note to yourself to quit trading around then. Numerous informal investors will, in general, lose cash in the time encompassing (and including) the New York lunch hour if trading U.S. markets. If you see this inclination, don't battle it. Quit trading during portions of the day you commonly lose cash. Help yourself to remember this when you start trading every day.

Have a Starting Position Size

If you exchange with a default position size, ensure it is set fittingly. Adding a digit to a position size could spell catastrophe. Dropping a digit implies exchanging a small amount of what you could have, and you pass up a chance.

Once you change your position size dependent on your entry point and stop misfortune areas, note your record balance before trading. A legitimate position measuring limits risk to a small level of record capital, for example, 2%. If you have a $40,000 account, you can risk up to $400 on an exchange.

Remember this greatest risk for the duration of the day (or compose a content note on your screen) to remind yourself this is the most you can risk on one exchange.

The Economic Calendar Must Be Considered

High effect monetary occasions can cause value spikes/holes, making critical slippage (the distinction between the value you expect and the value you get) on stop misfortune orders. It's ideal to abstain from being in exchanges for a couple of minutes encompassing high effect planned news occasion. Check your monetary schedule before trading and note the high effect news-times. For U.S. stocks and prospects, you can utilize Bloomberg. For Forex, look at the Daily FX financial schedule.

On the off chance that you exchange individual stocks all the time, check if the organization does not have income or different declarations due out that day. The Yahoo! Finance profit schedule functions admirably. Know about these occasions, to abstain from trading directly before the declaration.

Important Thoughts

Help yourself to remember your risky propensities and how you will deal with those circumstances should they emerge. Go over your Key Trading Thoughts.

Be Mindful as You Start Trading

You are set to exchange. This procedure should help dispense with certain errors identified with position size, trading an inappropriate record/contract, trading during news, or just not setting up your brain to exchange.

As you begin searching for potential exchange arrangements, remember your Key Trading Thoughts. This will help keep you out of awful exchanges (ones not in your trading plan) and keep your caution and prepared to jump on great chances.

Use the Right Trading Account

In Meta Trader and Ninja Trader (for instance), you can sign various records utilizing a similar stage. Ensure you are trading the right record. When you practice day trading in a mimicked record, yet additionally have live records. You would prefer not to have an incredible day, to acknowledge you traded in recreation rather than with genuine capital. In the event, that day trading prospects, ensure you are trading the rightmost noteworthy volume contract. Know about termination dates on the agreements you exchange.

Make a Trading Routine

Your day trading routine may shift marginally from this, contingent upon your trading style and the market you exchange. Make a daily schedule, however. It just takes about a moment or two to experience and can spare you from a great deal of dissatisfaction.

CHAPTER 8:

Day Trading

An important part of day trading is understanding the different options available to you, which will best suit your available time, finances, and interests. Although all-day trading activities seek to profit by purchasing stocks and selling them at a higher price within the same day; there are several different types of day trading:

Options

The two types of options are puts and calls. A stock option is a contract between two people. As the buyer of the option, you will purchase the right to buy shares from a different party at a set price within a set time frame. A call means you have the right to buy at the agreed price, while a put means you can sell.

If you are trading on the stock market, this can be very beneficial; you can purchase the option at a low price and wait for the price to rise. Once the price has risen, you can then complete the purchase by buying the shares and selling them immediately to someone else, making a profit along the way.

Day traders will often deal with the options, buying the right to buy shares from someone, and selling the option to someone else. In principle, this is the same as dealing in options on the stock market, but the risk is lower as you do not expend any funds until you find a buyer. The option to buy is yours, but this does not mean you have to.

Futures

One of the most approved options for many day traders and an excellent place for a beginner to start. On the stock market, a futures contract has been created between two parties; one agrees to sell a certain amount of stock to the other in the future, but the price is fixed at the time of the contract. These can be purchased and sold on the market as different speculators decide whether they can profit on the futures contract's maturity value.

Day trading in futures means that you are focusing on the future contracts and looking to buy and sell any which will turn you a profit within a day. Future trading is a good guide regarding the market and going in general; this makes it easier to trade in as they produce a more reliable picture of prices than many other trading types.

Currencies

When you are abroad and needed to change your money into another currency, you will already understand that currency rates vary daily. This volatility allows people to trade on two currencies of their choice and make a profit.

In simple terms, you seek to purchase a set amount of a certain currency, for example, 200 US$. This may cost you 150 GBP. If you then wish to change your funds back, the exchange rate may have moved. This results from market demand; the more popular a currency is, or the more the country's resources are needed, the better the exchange rate will be. If the US market improves, you may need to pay 175 GBP to get the same 200 US$. If you have already purchased the currency, you will change it back and make yourself a 25 GBP profit, less any transaction charges.

Day trading in currencies works on the same principles; you will be able to trade online with any currency worldwide and potentially make good profits. Of course, every trade involves you being a buyer and a seller; this does increase the risk.

Stocks

Shares are the first thing most people think of when considering the stock market. Purchasing shares and holding them for the long term to make money from increased value and dividends is a very successful tactic by many investors.

It is also possible to day trade in the same way; however, your window of opportunity is much smaller! Shares you purchase should be at the bottom of their fall or already on the way up. This should allow you to purchase some and then sell them again later the same day for a profit.

To successfully trade in stocks, you will need to keep a close eye on the stock market and which companies are performing well. The best ones to invest in are those who normally do well but have had a blip thanks to an unforeseen but fixable event. These shares will usually dip and then re-climb throughout the day.

Arbitrage

You need to be informed that there are many different markets, and you can trade in any of these. You can trade in more than one market simultaneously and make money doing so. This type of trading involves locating a product selling for less in one market than another. Once you have located the product, you purchase as many as possible in one market and sell them instantly in the other market. The risk is minimal as you hold the stock for only a few moments. The price difference needs to be enough to provide a small profit after allowing for the trade costs.

There are usually very small windows of opportunity available to make funds trading this way. The process of arbitrage helps to consolidate the prices across the different markets; it is an excellent way of keeping trading fair. It provides the opportunity to create a decent profit simultaneously, depending on how much you can afford to invest in the process.

Momentum Trading

Big companies can be hugely affected by news in either the wider economy or by events inside their business, but the information is publicly available. It is important to wait until you see the market movement.

Once you are certain that the share price is climbing or dropping, you will purchase your shares. Only buy as the share price climbs; the momentum builds. Generally, events like this will hit a share price and then naturally rebalance later in the day. So, it is essential to monitor the trend and sell when it starts to go back down.

Always buy in a rising (bullish) market and sell in a decreasing market (bearish). It is best to set yourself a target price. This should be at a level that will allow you to make a reasonable profit after allowing for buying and selling the transaction costs.

Swing Trading

It is natural for the price of any commodity to change during the day. Swing trading attempts to profit from these movements of prices. You need to identify the products or stocks which are moving throughout each day. At some point, they will go from higher to lower and then back again. Operating as a swing trader means buying at the low end of the swing and waiting for it to go back to the top end of the swing, all within a day's space. Remember that you do not need to buy and sell at the top and bottom of the swing; as long as the difference between the two prices will give you a profit and cover costs. Even a product with very small swings can be a good investment; small, consistent profits can quickly mount up.

No matter which option you choose to trade in, it is important always to have a professional approach and treat your day trading as a business. Many people have attempted day trading and lost substantial funds as they have not prepared or had the right approach. Any trading on the stock market requires research, patience, and understanding of how the stock market works. The more you know about your chosen market sector, the better you will predict the up and down movements and purchase the right day trading option for the occasion. It is possible to day trade in all the different options listed above; it is even possible to day trade as part of a larger investment strategy. The key is to be prepared!

No matter which type or types of trading you commit to, you should always sell and consolidate your position at the end of the day. The prices listed on the market can change dramatically overnight, and you will have little ability to recover your capital. You will only be able to watch your funds disappearing and hope they recover, to some extent, in the morning.

CHAPTER 9:

How Much Do Day Traders Make?

Day trading can sound exciting, and it certainly is. And if you have more significant amounts of capital to invest, and you're very good at it, then day trading can help you make large amounts of money over short periods. But if you are just getting started, how much can you earn day trading? Let's try looking at some realistic scenarios before having visions of millions of dollars.

The first thing to consider when trying to gauge the potential for success in any endeavor is the Pareto principle. This principle tells us that 20% of the people get 80% of the spoils. It doesn't matter what you're talking about, and you could be talking about farmers. In that case, 20% of the farmers will be responsible for 80% of the output. In the stock market, 20% of the investors will take 80% of the returns, which most certainly applies to day trading. Most days, traders will have to keep their day job, and many may end up losing their initial capital investment.

This isn't too out and out discouraging anyone from taking up day trading. Many factors will decide success or failure. For example, many people start off with high excitement levels when taking on something new, like day trading, but they quickly fizzle out. In short, they fail to put in the work required to excel. There would be a million reasons for it. Some people might wilt at the first sign of a challenge. Others may become bored with it. Some people are downright lazy—day trading takes work, and they were hoping for a get rich quick scheme.

Just like only a small percentage of basketball players are ever going to be NBA stars, only a tiny percentage of day traders are going to rise to become the cream of the crop and make millions of dollars. That said, you can take action to seriously tip the odds in your favor. After all, many people practice basketball with an all-out effort and become top-level players. Even if they aren't Kobe Bryant or Lebron James, they still may be very successful. The same principle applies to day trading. You may be a budding star or not—but if you dive in 100% to study the markets and finance and trading, you will significantly increase your odds. Even if you don't become a star, if you are a smart trader who hedges risk well, then you may be able to make a solidly upper-middle-class income from it even if you don't become a top-level trader.

One rule is that disciplined traders, at least in the long run, are going to make more money than people who are flying by the seat of their pants kinds of people.

The more capital you start with, the more money that you're going to make. But let's have a look at the minimum. Suppose that you start off with the recommended minimum amount of capital, which is $30,000.

Using leverage at 4:1 means you can potentially control $120,000 worth of stock. Remember that there is a 1% rule on risk per trade, and starting with $30,000, that means you'll be trading $300 at a time. Assuming you're a disciplined trader, you will have a good stop-loss strategy. Standard values are a win rate of 50% (that is, half your trades are profitable), and your winners are around 1.5 times bigger than your losers. These figures sound like no big deal, but it may take you a couple of years to get to this level. Now let's use these assumptions together with a guess that you make, on average, 5 trades per day or about 100 per month. With a 50% success rate, you'll have 50 profitable trades per month. A reasonable stop loss is $0.10, so with a 1.5 times ratio of the winner to the loser, you're making $0.15 per share in profits. You can control 3,000 shares per trade. So that gives you a monthly profit of $22,500. Your losses come from the stop loss figure of $0.10 a share, so you're going to lose $15,000 per month.

Your gross income will then be the difference, or $7,500 a month. However, remember that you'll need to pay lots of commissions. Brokers don't let you trade stock for free. In the end, your actual profit will probably be about $5,000 a month.

Now, this isn't bad to get started. So, you're able to work from home, doing something fun and exciting that is even a little bit risky, and make an OK middle-class income from it. But it's probably not the kind of income you were hoping to see.

That isn't to say that you can't grow your business over time and make huge amounts of money. You absolutely can do that. However, we're trying to show here that day trading isn't a get rich quick scheme. It's not dissimilar from any other kind of business that takes time, work, and energy to grow.

Of course, you might be better than average. If you are really good, maybe 65% of your trades turn out profitable, and you're banking $8,000–$9,000 per month depending on the size of commissions you have to pay. That's not an unrealistic possibility; however, remember that not everyone is as talented as anyone else. Some people are going to do worse than the 50% success rate that we initially started with, and in those cases, they will make less money, maybe a couple thousand a month or less. Still, more won't make anything, and some are going to end up with losses.

CHAPTER 10:

Designing a Trading Plan

You need to have a long-term plan of success that will serve as your reference guide, as well as a business plan.

Trading Plans

You'll hear a lot of trading gurus tell you to make a plan. Well, what exactly is a trading plan, and why do you need one? A trading plan by itself is not going to matter too much. However, when done right, it can help you focus and nail down your vision when it comes to trading.

Perhaps a more appropriate term for this is to call it a trading business plan instead of just a trading plan. Much like how you need to record all key information (both financial and in terms of vision) in your business plan, your trading plan needs to do the same for your trading business. At a minimum, it needs to have the following information:

Instruments to Trade

What instruments will you be trading? List them all out here. You can also list out the individual stocks you will be trading.

When starting, it's best to pick a single instrument and trade just that. The methods described here work for any instrument in any time frame.

This doesn't mean you go out and try to trade everything under the sun. You build a base with one, then two instruments, and then expand outward. Much like individuals, stocks have natures of their own in terms of liquidity and volatility. Some stocks have certain tendencies, depending on the time of the day.

You need to observe and learn all this to trade successfully and doing so one by one is the way to go about it.

Markets and Timing

Which markets will you be trading? When will you trade them? Most of you reading this will have full-time jobs or something else going on. So, you need to note down your session time and stick to it.

Which is the best session for beginners or busy people to trade? Well, there's no such thing as "best" to begin with. In terms of liquidity, the open is probably the best. The other side to this is that the volatility can be pretty extreme. Things pick up toward the end of the day as well, so it's not as if the open is the only worthwhile time to trade.

The afternoon session is usually seen as something of a graveyard, with many traders stepping out for lunch. Don't just assume this is so. Observe the market and check its tendencies. While the more active stocks tend to slow down quite a bit, some instruments provide easy pickings.

Risk Limits

What is your daily risk limit? Weekly, monthly, etc.? It is also a good idea to execute a gain-protection plan. What this means is that if you have a bunch of winners during the session (say two or more) or if you make a certain percentage of your account during the session (say anything about 0.5%), then you could decide to stop trading during that session if your gains dip below 0.25% or if you lose two more trades.

The idea is that you've made money during the session, and you would like to hang on to it. This is to protect a string of winners or a huge gain. Once you've had a great day, it's perfectly fine to set a lower loss limit to protect some of it so that no matter what happens, you'll end the day up.

Events

The markets have many external events that affect them, such as earnings announcements, dividends, splits, interest rate announcements, press conferences, and on and on. Generally speaking, you need to pay attention to the following events:

- Earnings.

- Special events of the individual stock or political events like elections.

- Interest rate announcements.

- Nonfarm payrolls (NFP).

That's it. These events are always scheduled in advance, and as a beginner, stop trading an hour before the announcement and resume an hour after it has passed. The reason is that volatility jumps like crazy, and your stops will get triggered.

If you have any positions open that are close to profit, take a lower profit just before the announcement, as long as it doesn't affect your risk numbers too much. Similarly, if you have a trade that is in a loss and is near its stop-loss, you have to close the trade out just before the event.

If your trade is in the middle of the road or is even break even, ride the event out and hope for the best. Some stocks are better than others in this regard. Stay away from flashy companies run by Twitter-wielding CEOs who tend to send their products into space instead of building profits. You know who I'm talking about.

Aside from being annoying, you can bet there will be several algorithms and bots tracking every character such people type into Twitter, and all it takes for a flash tumble to occur in the stock is a typo or a rash tweet. Stick to boring names no one has heard of, and you'll be much better off, no matter how much you love or hate the company.

Review System

Every successful trader spends a lot of time reviewing their trades and actions over the week. Mention the time you will spend reviewing.

Practice

When will you practice your skills? What skills will you practice? Each strategy has some skills you need to execute, not to mention mental skills. Set aside time to practice each of these individually to perfect it.

Journals

As important as your trading plan is, the document that is of primary importance for your trading success is your trading journal. This will list all the trades you took over the past week and serve as a record for you to review. In addition to written records, you should also save screenshots of your trades on entry and exit.

Remember to also save screenshots of the market condition on the higher time frame on trade entry. You will often notice how you might have misjudged the higher time frame action.

Below are the things your trading journal needs to record at a minimum:

- Date.

- Instrument (the ticker or name of the stock).

- Entry price.

- Stop-loss level.

- Stop distance.

- Position size.

- Reasons for entry (describe in as much detail why this entry was in line with your strategy and what you saw).

- Reasons or exit.

- Exit date.

- P/L.

- Mental state on entry.

- Mental state on exit.

You can either have this recorded on a spreadsheet or in a notebook; it doesn't matter where as long as you can review it easily. Save your screenshots in a numbered manner and appropriate folders. In addition to this, you can also record your screen and yourself during the session and review your demeanor and market action at the time of entry to verify whether you saw things correctly.

Remember, the more information you record at the time, and the more potential things there are for you to improve and learn.

Aside from the trading journal, you should also keep a mental journal. This is simply a record of what your mental state was during the session and if anything was bothering you at the time. It's up to you as to how much information you want to put in here, but you must aim to record whether you followed your preparation routines properly on that particular day.

Your prep routine can include physical exercise, meditation, visualization, affirmations, skill practice, and so on. It's up to you to decide what you want to include. Your aim should be to include things that are as repeatable as possible. Don't include too many things because you like its idea but will be stretched for time when it comes to implementing it.

The last journal you need to have is an assessment journal. You can incorporate this within your trade journal itself or as a separate document. When you're starting out, if it is logistically possible, I'd recommend reviewing your session after a thirty-minute break once it ends. This way, the action is still fresh in your mind, and you're more relaxed.

Go through all your trades and review the screenshots. Review the video recording as well to confirm and check if what you saw was true. Record what you did incorrectly and, even more importantly, record what you did right. The review is not just about finding things to improve; it's also about celebrating things you did right.

Doing a review after each trading session will increase your rate of improvement instead of doing it weekly. Remember, even a session where you place no trades should be reviewed for mental state and whether you were tuned in or zoned out. Did you miss any opportunities? Leave no stone unturned.

Training

Trading is a unique endeavor in that we spend more time in the market (that is, game day) than in practice. Every other high-performance activity requires a minimum of double the amount of time spent in practice than in games. So how do you achieve this when it comes to trading?

Well, first off, you're not going to be able to achieve anything like double the amount of practice time as trading time. However, by simply assigning time every day to practice and improve your skills and strategy, you'll be putting yourself way ahead of the curve.

Make at least 15 minutes every day to train your skills in simulation. Break down your strategy into its elements and practice each skill separately. You can also commit to practicing your skills in session if it happens to be slow or if there aren't any opportunities available.

Simulation software has a market replay feature, so you can simulate a market at a much faster pace and hone your skills instead of letting dead market time go to waste. Finally, schedule a month of each year or a couple of weeks off every quarter to review your existing skillset and to improve yourself as a trader.

Remember, do not trade every single day that the market is open. This is the easiest way to go insane. Take some time off and schedule breaks to keep yourself fresh.

Progression

Your progression should always be from simulation to demo and only then to live. You need to place at least 200 trades on the demo and make money from the demo before going live. It simply isn't worth it otherwise. Your practice should be done on simulation software to ensure you're keeping your skills fresh.

Once you've completed 200 trades on the demo and have made money on the instrument, you then add the next instrument on simulation and backtest your strategy on it. Once this passes, you demo trade it for 200 trades. Once you make money on this, you begin trading it live.

You first do it on simulation to see if it works any changes you choose to make to your system. If so, trade it on demo and compare it with your live results. If it is more successful, then push it live.

CHAPTER 11:

Money Management

Money management is how you handle your finances, your savings, your expenditure, and investments. It is making sure you can survive a financial crisis. It means planning a budget for your long-term goals and making investments to achieve your goals successfully. When you manage your money, you will be able to make wise purchases. Otherwise, you will always complain about having less money no matter how much your income is. It is known as investment management.

Money management is more about risk. When you have better money management skills, you will reduce the risk. You must understand all the areas of money management to avoid any risks—plan with a negative bias. Always asks yourself "what-if" scenarios, act, and technique. When budgeting for money management, make sure you are spending less than what you save. Excellent money management will help you monitor your spending before going beyond your budget. By doing this, you will secure your savings.

You will be able to invest if you make the right decisions. Avoiding taking on more risks will help you reach your financial goals. The strategies you use in your investments play a significant role in your success. When you decide to invest, the first important thing to focus on is the risk involved, and you can avoid it. Here are some of the basics, advantages, and disadvantages of money management.

The Basics of Money Management

Money management is a broad term that involves solutions and services in the entire investment industry. You can now have a wide range of resources in today's market and also phone applications to help you manage all your finances. Investors can also seek services from a financial advisor for professional money management. Financial advisors work with private banking and even brokerage services to offer money management plans involving retirement and estate planning services.

The Advantages of Money Management

Better Tracking of Your Money

When you have a reasonable budgeting plan, you can track how you use your money and monitor every expense. It is a significant benefit to you, as you can spend less and end up saving more money. Monitor your costs for some months and then change your budgeting by removing the less required payment and allocate that money to your savings plan, a retirement plan, or a vacation fund.

Excellent money management will help you stay on track; you will be able to pay your bills on time, will be able to stay within your limit, and avoid bank account overdraws. Poor money management can put you in bad debt quicker than a blink of an eye. You can prevent those nasty fees charges when you go over your limit. By having an excellent budgeting plan, you will avoid overspending.

A Good Retirement Plan

Better money management and savings programs will help you in the long term. You will be able to secure your future and have an excellent retirement plan. With better money management skills will give you a better retirement plan. No matter how much you save, even when you save and invest a small amount of money, it will provide you with a more significant amount for your retirement later in life.

Peace of Mind

Proper money management brings you peace of mind. Having bills on the counter and having no idea how you will pay the bills or not having the money to purchase something you needed. All these issues can be difficult to face each day. Managing your money wisely and experience all the benefits of sound money management, you will enjoy peace of mind, and you can provide for yourself and your family, too.

The Disadvantages of Money management

Rapid Changes

With the rapid changes in the financial world, it can change your management plans every time. It is sometimes challenging to adjust your planning to incorporate fast-changing situations. Unless your project can help to adopt the new techniques, it will be limited.

Time-Consuming

Managing your money can sometimes be a time-consuming exercise. It requires you to make the estimates as accurate as possible. However, you can use software and mobile applications to assist you with planning, and this may reduce the time you will take if you were not using the technologies. And if you have less knowledge about money management, it will take you more time to achieve this.

Inaccuracy

When planning, you make a lot of assumptions in terms of estimation of your expenses. Any shift like an economic downturn or the change in the currency rate or interest rates can change your planning estimates.

Why Is Money Management Important?

Money turns to wealth when it is well-managed. It is an instrument used to pursue wealth. For wealthy people, having and spending money does not bring them happiness, which gives them joy, a steady income, achieving their goals, and leaving a legacy to their loved ones.

Money management focuses on your habits, and your decision making can have affected the outcome of your long-term strategies. In pursuit of wealth, there are many powerful elements such as debts, risks, and taxes that can take away all the hard work you have put in to achieve your goals. It is a life skill that everyone must learn. You don't have to be financially savvy to start managing your money. There is plenty of information available to help you better understand your finances. The following are the importance of money management:

- **You are establishing clear goals.** Have a transparent approach to your decision in money management to build your wealth. Making the best decision will bring you closer to your goals. Also, set some clear and realistic goals you want to achieve and set a time horizon to perform them. Setting up clear goals will help you track where you are, and this will help you see your progress towards your goals. Some people give up earlier due to not being able to see their progress. You can see your progress and stay encouraged if you break your goals into short term milestones. Finally, have clear and quantifiable goals to help you to make clear decisions. Abandon any choices that will not get you closer to your destination.

- **You are controlling your cash flow.** Spend less than what you earn will help you accumulate wealth.

  You can't be financially successful if you are not tracking and monitoring your expenditure. Drawing up a spending plan and religiously following the program might seem trivial, but it's central to the world's wealthiest people's success.

If you own a business, your goal will be to increase your monthly profits, which you will invest in for more growth. You will learn how to prioritize your spending when you have a solid money management plan and make the right decisions, which will bring you closer to your goals.

- **Budgeting.** Creating a household income budget is an essential part of personal money management. Budgeting will help you better understand your cash flow, thus giving you a clear understanding of your current financial situation.

- **Debt management.** There is proper financial education to help you understand consumer debt and how it works. Financial advisers and credit counselors advise how you can review your debts, your loan terms, and how you can pay off the debt quickly and stress-free.

- **You are managing your risks.** Your risk exposure increases as you continue accumulating your wealth. You might think that wealth can make life easier, but it does not. The ignored reality is that it can make life more complicated. You are getting a bigger house, expensive cars, and lavish lifestyles. These bring financial exposure and the potential to lose if all is great.

Have a risk management assessment in your money management plan with protection strategies to prepare you for the unexpected. Some of the unintended exposure include:

o   Income loss due to illness or accident

o   Death of the breadwinner in the family

o   Asset exposure to liability claims

Money management will provide you with a 360-degree view of your financial status and having financial discipline will help you overcome these obstacles. With a solid money management principle, you will have better control of your financial goals.

- **You are taxing efficiently.** Paying taxes is a responsibility; however, there is no obligation to spending more than necessary. Most people are not aware of how much taxes they are paying and unnecessary taxes and how it affects their wealth accumulation abilities. Money management does not focus on what you make but what you get after paying your taxes. Consider the tax characteristics of your investment and your overall portfolio. The first thing to consider is the account location, the money allocation on different accounts based on respective tax treatment. Secondly, the asset location, wherein you allocate different types of investments among the different types of funds on the tax treatment, giving your least tax-efficient assets to a tax-deferred account such as 401(k).

The taxable accounts can hold in a tax-efficient investment such as low turnover funds. It will give you more income distribution options in the more tax-efficient retirement, thus enabling you to accumulate more wealth faster.

CHAPTER 12:

Better Options Trading

A trading scheme of options is a mechanism for creating and selling signals using a validated stock analysis tool.

The program can be based on some alternative approach and includes both basic and technical evaluations. Options trading systems may concentrate on changes in the underlying stock price, interest, decay time, unusual purchasing/selling behavior, or a mix.

Essentially, it is a checklist of conditions that must be met before entering the trade. When all conditions are fulfilled, a signal is produced to buy or sell. The criteria for each type of options trading strategy are different.

Whether it's long calls, covered calls, bear spreads, or naked index options, each has its type of trading system. An optional salt trading program can help you get out false signals and create trust in entries and exits.

How Relevant Is a Trading Network for Options?

The demand for options is very complex. Trading without a framework is like building a house without a plan. Movements of price, time, and stock will all impact your earnings. You must be mindful of each of these variables. Emotion can easily be swayed as the market shifts.

With a program, the response to these natural and usual emotions can be controlled. How much did you sit and watch a trade losing money when your order was filled?

Have you seen a stock price spike when you think of buying it? It is important to have a clear strategy in place to make rational and reasonable trade decisions. You can boost your trade executions by designing and following a good program, as emotionless and automatic as a machine.

Advantages of Trading Scheme Options

- **Leverage:** Selling options have the stock market leverage. You can manage hundreds or thousands of shares with options at a fraction of the stock price itself.

  A change in stock values from 5–10% may be equivalent to an increase of 100% or more. Seek to focus on percentage gains against dollar losses in your exchange. It needs a radical shift in traditional thinking, but it is necessary to effectively manage the trading system.

- **Objectivity:** A successful trading scheme of options is focused on observable parameters that allow signals to be bought and sold. It takes the subjectivity of your business so that you can focus on predetermined variables that trigger explosive trade.

- **Flexibility:** Most options traders can tell you that options give your trading flexibility. The demand for options makes it remarkably easy to take benefit of short-term positions.

  You may build strategies for overnight gains with clearly specified risk with earnings events and weekly options. There are ways to benefit from the trend to the range of any market situation.

- **Security:** The options trading program will serve as a hedge against certain investments, depending on an acceptable strategy in prevailing market conditions. This is a way of using defensive puts.

- **Risk:** The trading structure of good options reduces the risk in two essential ways. Cost is the first method. The option prices are very small relative to the same quantity of inventory. The second way issues end. A successful system will easily reduce losses and keep them low.

  The more tools in your toolbox, the more able you are to adjust business conditions. Unless the markets were to act in the same way every day, trading would become a play for children. To start designing your options trading, you have to build a trading strategy or strategy to lead you in the right direction.

  Start with the basic framework and tweak it to identify and enhance your trading criteria.

It takes time and experience to develop a productive options trading program that can return 100% or more in consistently profitable businesses. If you are pleased with your machine parameters, you can look at your own program's automatic trading.

Steps to Options Trading System

- **Pick a strategy:** You can select any strategy to start developing a program. The best way to get going is to buy calls and puts. You will add new approaches to your trade to boost your method by researching and understanding more about how prices move.

  Adding long-term equity protected calls and protections is a sensible next step so that you can debit your account by generating a monthly or weekly cash flow.

- **Trade:** It is time to trade once you have established the fundamentals of your strategy. Start small contracts, one or two contracts, and keep detailed transaction records. Be sure to include the underlying inventory price at the time you purchased or sold your right.

  Notes will allow you to evaluate how and where you can change. When you add new trading requirements to your system, your statistics should be strengthened. If not, it is time to re-evaluate your given criteria.

- **Measure-assess the successes and shortcomings:** The duration of the research depends on the amount you traded. If you trade actively, it is important to have a weekly or monthly summary.

  Compare your winnings to your losses. Zero on the main factors that make up a good trade and seek to change your parameters to boost your results.

  Analyze your mistakes as frustrating as they can be. Tune the requirements to avoid the same errors again. Analyzing your errors is as critical, if not more, to research your productive businesses.

- **Change:** If there is a losing streak or spot in your options trading scheme, change it. Adjust it. It's no shame to be wrong. This is part of the trading industry. The irony is that you are blind to and repeat your mistakes.

  You will keep the device in line with changing business patterns and conditions by identifying the blind spots and making modifications. It sounds so basic, but perseverance and discipline are important.

- **Know:** A method of trading is not static. Keep your mind engaged by learning always. The more you research the stock market and the trading system of options, the more you learn and the better.

CHAPTER 13:

How to Become a Top Trader?

You are the one responsible for turning your venture into foreign exchange into a successful endeavor. That is one of the great things about the stock. You do not have a boss screaming down your neck, telling you to do something you do not agree with. You can come up with your trading plan based on your own research and your knowledge. That being said, success can come more quickly for some than for others, and a lot of the time, this has to do with approaching this endeavor with the right strategy. We will provide you with three strategies designed to help you make this stock as profitable as possible (with as little loss as possible):

Strategy 1. Buy Low and Sell High

If you began stock trading today with $25,000 in your pocket and access to a trading platform, all ready and raring to go, how would you know what is low and what is high? It's your first day. Naturally, for you to understand what would represent a good low investment and conversely what is high, you need to know the exchange rate history of that currency. Maybe the exchange rate for the Japanese yen seems low, but actually, compared to last year or a few months ago, it's a little high.

Now it would not be a good time to buy.

Maybe the pound seems low right now, but yesterday the British government announced that the first round of the Brexit negotiations with the EU failed and therefore the pound may have room to go lower than it is was when you logged onto your trading platform. You can wait and see what the pound is today or tomorrow and buy then.

The point here is that buying low and selling high requires understanding the patterns associated with that stock and what might cause it to go up or down. And that's merely the buying side of things. Once you have bought low, you need to figure out when you are going to sell. This is where a good trading plan will come into play. A good plan will prevent you from selling too soon, or even not selling soon enough.

Strategy 2. Focus on Not Losing Money Rather Than on Making Money

This may not be an easy strategy to understand initially, in part because not losing money and making money seem like two sides of the same coin. They are, but they are not identical. One of the personality types that is associated with difficulty in finding success in trading is the impulsive type. This type of person wants to make money and they want to make it quick. They have a vague strategy about how they plan on doing that, but the most important thing to them is that they have a high account balance to make as many trades as they need to turn a profit. This is the wrong approach. Currencies are not the same as stocks.

A stock's value may change very little even over a week, so the strategy that involves a lot of trades to make money is usually not the best strategy.

You need a clear idea of when you are going to but, yes, because you want to make money, but mostly because you don't want to lose.

Every market that involves exchanges, like the stock market, has some implicit risk, and stock trading is risky, too, because you may be tempted to give up the advantage you have to try and make money quickly.

Strategy 3. Develop a Sense of Sentiment Analysis

Alright, the third strategy was going to be about Fibonacci retracement, which is a type of technical analysis of the market, but as this is the basics of stock trading, we are going to go into a different strategy that is not any easier than a Fibonacci retracement, just different. Sentiment analysis is a term that is used in many different specialties, not just finance, and it is not easy to describe.

It is essentially a type of analysis that is not based on a chart showing exchange rates over time (technical analysis) or understanding a factor that might today be affecting the value of the stock (fundamental analysis). Sentiment analysis attempts to gauge the tone of the market, the direction the market is heading in, by parsing all of the available information.

A key to understanding sentiment analysis is likening it to public opinion. The economy may be booming, people have more money in their pocket, so this hypothetical country's stock should increase in value, but maybe it doesn't. Maybe there is something that is causing the market to be bearish, which might cause the stock to drop.

As you perhaps can tell, as this analysis is not based on any concrete information, it can be thought of as intuitive and no one has intuition on the first day. Let's be honest about that. Intuition comes from experience. But the purpose of this strategy is to introduce to you the idea that not the foreign exchange market, like any market is not going to behave like a machine because it's not a machine.

Markets are places where human beings come together and humans are unpredictable, often in a frustrating way. Perhaps one day, stock trading may be handled by machines (that wouldn't be fun), but that day is far off and so you will have to develop your own sense of where the market seems to be going and use this as a strategy to achieve success in this endeavor.

Regardless of the investment that you make, be sure always to do your research. Doing research is a must. It is what will increase your chances of making the right investment decision.

The more that you understand something, the more likely that you will be able to predict how it will move in the market. This is why doing research is essential. It will allow you to know if something is worth investing in or not. Remember that you are dealing with a continuously moving market, so it is only right that you keep yourself updated with the latest developments and changes. The way to do this is by doing research.

Whether you will start forex trading or trade in general, it is always good to have a plan. Make sure to set a clear direction for yourself. This is also an excellent way to avoid being controlled by your emotions or becoming greedy. You should have a short-term plan and a long-term plan. You should also be ready for any form of contingency.

Make your plans practical and reasonable. Remember that you ought to stick to whatever project you come up with, so be sure to keep your ideas real. Before you come up with an idea, you must first have quality information. Again, this is why doing research is very important.

What if you fail to execute your plan? This is not uncommon. If this happens to you, relax and think about what made you fail to stick to your plan? Was it favorable to you or not? Take some time to analyze the situation and learn as much as you can from it. Indeed, having a plan is different from executing it. It is more challenging to implement a plan as it demands that you take positive actions.

Learn From Your Competitors

Pay attention to your competitors and learn from them. Studying your competitors is also an excellent way to identify your strengths and weaknesses. You can learn a great deal from your competitors, especially ideas on how you can better improve your business.

Your competitors can also help you promote your trading goals and draw more techniques. This way, you get a better idea of how to trade. You do not have to fight against your competitors; you can work together.

It is prevalent for people online to support one another. It is a good practice that you connect with other traders, especially those who are in the same niche. Do not think of them as your direct competitors, and you might be surprised just how friendly they can be.

Now, a common mistake is to consider yourself always better than others. This is wrong as you are only deluding yourself, making you fail to see the bigger picture. Instead of still seeing yourself better than your competitors, learn from them, and see how you can use this knowledge to improve your trading endeavors.

Cash-Out

Some people who trade forex or invest in cryptocurrency commit the mistake of not making a withdrawal. The reason why they do not cash out is so that they can grow their funds. Since you can only earn a percentage of what you are trading/investing, having more funds in your account means making a higher profit return. Although this may seem reasonable, it is not a recommended approach. It is strongly advised that you should request a withdrawal. You should understand that the only way to enjoy your profits truly is by turning them into cash; otherwise, it is only as if you were using a demo account. Also, by making a withdrawal, you lower your risks, since the funds you withdraw will no longer be exposed to risks.

You do not have to remove all your profits right away. If you want, you can withdraw 30% of your total profits, allowing the remaining 70% to add up to the funds in your account. The important thing is to make a withdrawal still now and then.

Take a Break and Have Fun

Making money online can be exciting and fun but it can also be a tiring journey. Therefore, give yourself a chance to take a break from time to time. When you take a break, do not spend that time thinking about your online business.

Instead, you should spend it to relax your body and clear your mind. You will be more able to function more effectively if you do this. This is an excellent time to go on a vacation with your family or friends or at least enjoy a movie night at home. Do something fun that will put your mind off of business for a while. Do not worry; after this short break, and you are expected to work even more.

Making money online is a long journey, so enjoy it. Making money online can be lots of fun. Do not just connect with people to build a good following, but also try to make friends with your connections. You do not have to take things too seriously. Keep it fun and exciting.

Conclusion

Options trading is a form of financial speculation that allows investors to buy or sell stock options without owning the underlying stock. This tends to result in much higher returns than investing in stocks directly.

One of options trading's biggest benefits is that it does not require a great deal of initial capital. Even a small sum can be used to buy stock options. However, the cost can quickly add up if large quantities are traded. The monthly premium will need to be paid using the profits generated when the option is exercised.

Options trading is thought to be the more sophisticated form of investing because it allows you to trade for price moves rather than simply for the stock itself. It requires more knowledge and understanding of the market.

To use options trading, you must predict how a stock or index will move in the future and what the potential price range is for that move.

Even though these strategies often work well for experienced traders, they can backfire if you are not prepared for losing money while trading. If you choose to trade options, you should do so only after getting professional advice and guidance from a licensed financial advisor or broker.

Although it might sound complicated, options trading is very straightforward and can be learned quickly with a little guidance from professional traders.

With options, there are several different trading platforms and strategies you can choose from. You must choose the type of trading which suits your personality the most.

If you're a beginner or live in an area with high stock market volatility, then I'd recommend that you stick to only index options and invest in only stocks for a while. This way, you can test out your options trading capability without the added risk of losing your money.

www.ingramcontent.com/pod-product-compliance
Lightning Source LLC
Chambersburg PA
CBHW071718210326
41597CB00017B/2521